Tending the Fig Tree

Vicki Grometer Jahns

March 2005
Cincinnati, Ohio

ISBN 1-59196-945

March 17, 2005

Cincinnati, Ohio

with thanks to
Diane Karampas
Daniel Jahns
Beth Thomas
The Tuesday Group

From Musings
Part One

On Grace
Part Two

Of Nature
Part Three

With Relationships
Part Four

Introduction
The Necessity of Poems

From Musings

Uncaptured Thoughts
If I Could Stop Time
Traces
What I Need to Most Understand Is Why
Bookends
Balance
Find Your Gift
Women Friends
New Year Old Year
Afternoon
Images for a Modern Woman
Rituals
Road Lines
Wisdom's Child
Gifts
Beauty

Fishback Creek
Don't Wait
No Purple for Me
The Young Perch on the Stools Together
The Tao of Us
Ashley
Ambiguity
the End of the Whip
Relationships and Roles
Life

On Grace

My Gnostic Side
Shekinah Thoughts
Dive in
When Maeve Was Three
On Making Decisions
Tightly Wrapped
A Poem for my Friend in Sorrow
The Sparrow
God's There
Where Are the Prophets?
The Veil in America
The Mark of Cain
Creation Midrash
At Crack of Dawn

Of Nature

Daylight
Silence
A Thought of Conservation
The Sky Hangs Heavy with Gray
The Trees that Block the View
The Muse
Sons of Thunder - daughters of the Mist
Abraham's Wish
Mazatlan
The Softness of Spring
Spring Storm
In the City
Choices
The Midwest
Many Layers Showing

With Relationships

Old Marriages
The Two of Us
Chalking the Walk
A Bit of Space
The Grandmother's Thread
Grief
Do Not Be Afraid to Love
Maeve's Magic Wand
Sustaining
A Mother's Job
Boys and Girls
Centered

The Necessity of Poems

There is a certain rhythm
to a poem.
It rocks one gently,
as a mother might.
Her arms wrapped
around an infant
struggling with the
newness of life out
of the womb.
It rolls itself against
the hard surface
of a rough world.
Softening the edges as
waves turn stone to sand.

Comfort comes from the
use of familiar words.
They fill the hollow places
causing emptiness and
yearning to subside,
For a while, for a while.

There is a certain rhythm
to a poem
It brings back universal
memories of man
connecting to man.
Similar emotions, shared
yearnings met with
companionship.

A poem, lest we forget,
calls us to reach
beyond ourselves into
the future, past the
stars, beyond the daily.
Poetry, hear the call,
bring gentle words
to mankind all.
*

From Musings

Part One

Un-captured Thoughts

Capturing thoughts is
difficult
They fly by fast.
Like a jet plane.
In the sky.

Out of the clouds.
Across the clearing.
And
Gone – gone to who knows where.

Into the shadows they go,
or vaporized for all eternity,
or waiting for the sun to bring
them back to view again.

Does someone else find them?
Do they send them on?
Will every thought I've ever had
be thought again upon?

Capturing thoughts is difficult.
They come before you know.
Keeping a thought in focus is
as hard as letting one go.
*

If I Could Stop Time

If I could stop time,
it might be right now
the late day quiet of an ordinary day.

No plans.
No phones ringing.
No schedule.
Only the silent house
whispering serenely to me.

Bees swarming.
Stillness.
The perfume of spring flowers.
Spring changing to summer as I watch.

If I could stop time
the only thing more I would wish for
is you by my side.
*

Traces

Girlish ways in older women,
traces of the beauty young

Seen still in the image
of maturity, sincerely won.

Grow young girls. Enjoy.
Youth's benefits are great.

But treasured most of all,
by me, are the years
of life come late.
*

What I Need Most to Understand is Why
Remembrance of the Holocaust

Why should we remember
sad things from the past?
I was asked.

Things we are not proud of,
and that hurt us still.
Why should we remember them?
Why give them voice if they were evil?

Why re-create the pain?
Where is the answer here?

At first it seems we do it
so we don't echo our mistakes.
We do it for the children
so they don't repeat our aches.

We do it for the memory of those
we lost and loved.
We do it to increase our
own capacity for caring.

Compassion, empathy, and ethics
are difficult to teach.
The core of those feelings
deeply form within.
We tell the stories over so we find
a way to begin.

Once again.
*

Bookends

Here we sit.
Two friends.
Like bookends
on the ends
of the events of
life.

Holding life between us.
Keeping events in their
places.
I look at you
and see the
wisdom
reflected in
our faces.
*

Balance

If yesterday is what
determines the day ahead,
I have already lost,
My freedom tossed,
a throwback to yesterday.
If only circles chart my course,
and round and round I go
I lose the butterflies of opportunity
that lead me on, you know.
But if I see only forward thrust
I chance to lose the wisdom
gained by practice,
patience, grace, and trust.

So both I need;
the circle and the line,
to focus on the unlimiting divine.

So may I move from yesterday
With wisdom following, too,
And greet undiscovered tomorrow
with hope for something new.

Find Your Gift

Everybody has a gift.
If you don't try
how would you know -
Run the race, jump the hurdle,
paint away like an old Van Gogh.

Everybody has a gift.
It is yours alone.
It's not your brother's or your friend's
It's yours to have and own.

Find your gift.
Find what you like to do.
But remember now to
try a lot of things before you're through!

Everybody has a gift.
Every soul a place.
Some of us will dream our time
And some of us will race.

Treasure gifts of yours
Treasure gifts of mine
Turn on creative energy
And honor earth divine.
*

Women Friends

Women,
once they are friends,
blend with each other to produce
uniqueness.

Looking back, life paints its magic,
bringing to the vision of the
wiser woman the knowledge
that so few of the details matter.

Moments of
absolute intensity are
no longer so vivid.

Like mothers who forget the groans of
childbirth,
so women forget the clashes
that separated them from
each others affection.

There is comfort in community.
Values need not
be explained, because they
are known, a common knowing,
bearing shades of black and white
that are now observed in
many shades of
exquisite gray.

Watching changes in ourselves
as we celebrate the changing faces of
our friends.

Connection and relationships,
shared memories, keep us
blended colors in the canvas
that illustrates our lives.

Women friends in a glorious array of
hues.
Highlighting each others strengths.
Yet every part of the canvas
true to itself alone.

New Year Old Year Many Years

I am beginning to understand
It's all about separation
and mending.
Leaving and coming.
Distancing and reuniting.

There is a glue that
binds - "forgiveness"
I believe is the glue.

Coming together.
Moving apart.
Going away.
Returning. Returning. Returning.

Maybe "time" is the glue,
just "time."
*

Afternoon

There before us
stretched the long hours
of the afternoon.
Meal over. Dishes done.
Services tucked away
into the morning
activity and
before us now lays
the rest of the day.

Birds arc in lazy movements,
gliding low,
in the ebbing heat.
Sighs release from human kind
as evening time we meet.

Sunday, and the clouds
are slower in the heavens.
The light's more pale from
the sun.
Quiet fills the afternoon
as reluctantly day is done
*

Images for a Modern Woman

I cannot run with the gray
   wolf to her forest den
I cannot conjure up the moon
   with owls in a piney glen.
I cannot dive to the depths of lake
   like the musky and the perch.
I cannot call from the
   lake side nest of eagle, duck, or loon.
I cannot hear in the deepest
   woods all sounds there are to know.
I cannot forage on the shore,
   like a chipping sparrow or crow.

But share I can in hiding
   my cubs in a safe, protected
   den.
And point I now to the cold
   white moon
   consistent in its rise.
And plunge I will into feelings deep
   that swim within the soul.
And call I will from the lakeside nest
   to bless my babies with all the best.
And in the deepest, deepest
   woods, I'll listen
   for their cries
And respond to them with
   mothering love
that clears the darkest skies.
                    *

Rituals

Rituals give order
to the threat of chaos
as we experience the events
that mark the time
in any given life.

They form us.
They honor us.
They comfort us.
They provide us with a sense of security
knowing that others have
passed this way
and have remembered
and honored that passing.

Rituals bring forth the symbols
by which we recognize ourselves
within each other.

Road Lines

The road workers have lined the side
of the road
between the pavement
and the grass median
with crushed gravel.

It is very tidy today.
Perhaps a factor of its newness.
Does it lead us on to adventure
Or does it keep us from straying?

I guess we'd have to know
only for ourselves.
Stay within the lines of tried,
or use lines as a birth shoot
to vistas, open wide.
*

Wisdom's Child

It's Wisdom's Child I seek
within my soul.

Seeing without language,
rules, or creed.

Using ceremony,
liturgy, to bring
me closer
to unity
with wisdom.

Come Wisdom's Child
and fill me
with the knowing
that strengthens me
to be
a human,
fully being.
*

Gifts

I can never give enough,
and that leads me to the wound
deep in my heart
of not fulfilling expectations.
Failure. Guilt.

So much more can I
respond to praise. Give
what I can give
from gladness,
and a sense of sharing.
Generosity brings on joy,
no matter how tiny the gift.

To be able to give,
with joy,
is a warm feeling that spreads
from the heart
to the contented place that
fills the soul with the meaning of life.

But spontaneity, not duty,
Happiness, not guilt,
Makes the giving grow and flower,
rather than a gift, begrudged,
whose blooms will quickly wilt.
*

Beauty

Lovely things are valuable
for their beauty.
Bridges may be needed.
Food must be grown.
Beauty, however, stands alone.

Some things are lovely.
We need those things.
Beauty is the best of all
to furnish souls with wings.

Starkness, darkness,
Weary and fatigued.
Broken, aching,
yearning.

Beauty brings renewal.
Softness. Shades of gentle
color. Respite and
repose.

Come lovely things
be by my side
as I walk the path of life
with purposeful
and patient stride.
*

Fishback Creek

I tell ya' she wanted all
the people connected
to her life to come sit
with her
like little paper dolls.

She fussed with their outfits.
Re-arranged their frilly little skirts.
Checked their posture.
And re-tied their hair bows.

Some she would send out for Ice Cream
to eat in little bowls with
pink flowers accompanied by
small spoons
with a well worn sheen.

As the evening grew cool she'd offer
lap robes to those who still
enjoyed the sun's setting.

Then off to bed, tidy and fine, to
re-emerge a refreshed paper doll
ready for the next day's engagement.
Perhaps, little cakes with ice cream
today, for a change?
*

Don't Wait

Don't wait.
Please don't wait.
I do not want to be missing
When you praise me.
I do not want to be gone,
Forever, when you miss me.
I do not want to be forgiven
All my transgressions
After death –
I want that now.

I do not want you to publish
post-humously my poems.
I do not want a party for me that I can't attend.

It is today that all my life needs seeing.
Today, I need know the reasons for my being.
*

No Purple for Me

When I was young my favorite
Color was red – passion,
Energy, direct thoughts,
Filling the world with my color.

In the middle of my life I found
Orange. It enveloped me and brought
a little depth of color to
the ordinary. It spread like a
low spot in the sand of the beach, filling with water,
reflecting the sunset to include in my boundaries
those dear ones that I loved
and shared with, in the daily routine of life. It
gave me space and personhood
separate from the multi-colors of my family.

Now I'm older. An older woman.
Full. Round. Lively. Wanting
my energy to stay within a smaller space. Finding the
whole world within me in
my daily routines, my simple pleasures. A space that
takes in new learning

everyday but has less need
to share the passion of that, and more interest in
observing
as others fill the paths with burning energy.
A quieter presence, powerful
Within its self.
Looking out.
Seeing the reds and oranges of my children
as they grow.
Watching the world with
interest and passion, in a
perspective that chooses
carefully how to blend,
when to influence,
when to turn up the heat to a
flicker of red again.

Now, older, my favorite color
Is pink with opalescent pearl tones.
Soft. Mellow. Kind.
Internalized. Growing.
Radiating back
To the world the reds and
Oranges necessary for them before they too
Reach pink and become translucent.
*

The Young Perch on the Stools Together

The young perch on the stools together,
holding their dinner plates in their laps.
Those who are older sit in the chairs,
close to the tables which help hold their plates.

I can see beauty in the young.
Fresh faces with clearly defined, sharp features.
An expectant look.
A confidence of their place in the life that lays
before them.
Invulnerability, stemming from lack of
accumulated disasters.
Competence, challenge, laced with physical
strength.

I can see beauty in the old.
Complex faces with gently defined, softened
features.
A knowing look.
A confidence of their contribution to the life that
lays behind them.

Vulnerability, stemming from accumulated
disasters.
Competence, softness, laced with experience.

The young plumply fill out their bathing suits at the pool.
They dress with nonchalance in front of mirrors.
They wear the high cut styles in underwear.
Those who are older plump out parts
of their bathing suits,
while other parts droop a bit.
They dress facing their lockers,
or behind curtained space.

At the pool, the beauty of the young is in their
physical being.
At the pool, the beauty of the old is in their bravery
and perseverance.

Young, old, women all,
What wonders we possess,
With bodies strong,
With hearts so full,
With love that takes no rest.
*

The Tao of Us

Looking to the Chinese
Taoist thought of yang and yin -
the source of all Harmony within
being the integration of the two-

I think of me.
I think of you.

How blest I am that you
pull back from anger, just.
That you can hold the balance.
That you sustain my trust.

How careless I, to joke when given news,
That brings to me the sincerity
of your most honest views.

For truly life's a balance.
A give and take and tweak.
A constant integration of
the harmony we seek.

The two of us are sometimes one,
although we each remain,
As individual as tiny flowers
Fed by springtime rain.

Ashley,
a heroine for my time.

She opened the car door and
he was there at her side.
Where did he come from?
What did he need?
Was it a gun he pointed at her?

In her apartment he tied her up.
With her tape he closed her mouth.
Her eyes alone could speak to him.

From within her self
she brought up to the openings of her soul
the peace that fed her spirit,
the love that calmed her grief.
He unbound her.
He pulled the tape from lips
that stayed calm
in response.
She began to tell him,
with respect, her story.

I have a little daughter.
Her Daddy died in my arms.
I know the agony of restlessness.
I know the hopelessness of despair.

For a moment on earth we can be
together,
together in our grief.
Redemption is our story.
Strength comes from my belief.

If you remember only one thing,
let it be that
you are loved by God in
Heaven
and in God you
will find peace.

He said she was an angel.
They rested in the quiet.
He asked if she would look into his eyes.
He said, "I am a dead man."

Redemption is our story.
There is a purpose here.
You and I together
for a moment in time.

She brought the talk back to herself.
What is my purpose?
Why am I here?
Why did you pick me to hide you?
What is my purpose?

He said again,
You are an angel.
An angel of the Lord.
Redemption is our story.
This little bit of time in peace
has given me the courage
to let you live.
Your purpose is my story.

Calmly then she walked away.
Out of the door of her house.
And soon enough, his freedom was rescinded
and he was the captive, justly bound,
with a hope of peace,
and redemption, newly found.
*

Ambiguity

Strong, swift, sure
Cowboys riding on the range
Decisions made in just a moment
Beliefs clear and true
One path so admired
Strong, swift, sure

Uncertain, dealing with ambiguity
Physicists exploring on the edge
Decisions revised as information arrives
Positions clear and changing
Uncertain, dealing with ambiguity

The baseball player swings his bat.
His goal is clear
No doubt of that
Get that ball up in the stands
Run the bases, strike up the bands.

But life, as it strikes me this day
Is not so clear in how to play.
What might be murky stays that way
and juggling this and that, I pray,
that decisions made will be "OK".

The End of the Whip

As the skaters turned -
he held his grip.
As down the icy lake they flew -
he held his grip.
As the leader turned
and made sharper the arc -
he held his grip.

When his turn never came to
move up the line,
when others continued to skate -
he lost this grip.

He spun from the line,
his skates in control,
his balance askew to
his will.

Across the ice his body flew
the last man in the line.
And where he landed,
they never knew.

As the skaters turned -
he held his grip,
the new skater at the end of
the skate line whip.
*

Relationships and Roles

Watch with me now. And listen, too.
Listen to the timbre change of voice.
Browse your eyes over body
language that clearly
states its choice.

Center to the problem is:
If I understand the
role I am to play with you, we can progress.
If you have no role for me
to play against,
my role I cannot guess.

If you're my spouse, companionably I speak,
my granddaughter with delight I greet.
my aging Mom with sympathy I bend,
a co-worker I know how to "Hey!"
and likewise, "Halloo" a friend.

But, never having met you,
and knowing not my role,
I must avert my eye contact and wait to see.
Is it respect you want from me?
Or do I need to guard my place as
authority and judge
and keep my face?

How hard it is to meet someone
and keep the channel clear
to know them as they really are,
and not just as they appear.

Watch with me now. And listen , too.
Listen to the timbre change of voice.
Meet me as a person who
can meet you back without the role,
and love you from the simple soul,
that every human is.
*

Life

It all comes down
to such a few things:

Being known for yourself
not for the many labels
or groups you are as a part of yourself;

Having more in common
with others than
not in common with others;

Recognizing the spark of
holiness in the earth,
in man,
in ideas,
in animals,
in inventions,
in imagination;

And, the satisfaction of a
good deed done by day's end.
*

Morning Watch

In the morning watch,
before the sun arises,
God's kiss the earth receives.
And then among
the sleeping are surprises.
He who dreams of peace believes.
*

On Grace

Part Two

My Gnostic Side

Oh, yes. I know.
Just do.
No doubt.
Can't explain it.

Man of modern thought with
rationale for every function
Cannot persuade me off
the path which divides
at this junction.

What I know, I know.
There is a God.
It doesn't matter
the facts of human story
God exists past mankind's glory.

There is a God. I know.
Just do.
No doubt.
Can't explain it.

Man of ancient traditions with
pictures clear of God
cannot convince me of
an old, wise male
who either sits in whimsical judgment or
pours out unconditional love
beyond the pale.

What I know, I know.
There is a God.
In the questions,
between the cracks of the concepts.
there is a God
that I cannot paint a picture of,
that I cannot explain.

A God who is beyond rules, logic, emotions.
A God who brushes by,
just a whisper in our brain.
*

Shekinah Thoughts

Ishtar morning star
First of day to rise
Bring to us our womanliness
and meet us in your skies.

Men removed from daily tasks
like God enthroned above
Need women to connect with
them and stir the Shekinah love.
like God enthroned above
Need women to connect with
them and stir the Shekinah love.

From city gates,
from crossroads,
from mountain tops on high,
the women come to speak their truths
And offer wisdom with a sigh.

Justice, mercy,
healing
Kindness, care for earth,
The wisdom of the mothers
Born again
at every persons birth.

God who perches
On a throne,
God whose robes
With jewels are sown,
Is not the God
who gives to me the comfort
that I need.

I pull from the goddess image
When I am in despair
From stories, food,
And caring,
From tenderness and
earthly beauty fair.

Not judgment, but compassion,
Not threats, but love so dear
Can heal my heart together
In a love that I can hear.
*

DIVE IN

Dive in.
Dive in to the center.
Dive in to the gong meditation.
Dive in to the still pool of water that is your inner self.

Get to know.
Get to know the stranger.
Get to know the stranger that is yourself.
Get to know the wisdom that rests within the soul
Of the stranger that is yourself.

Forgive.
Forgive that internal being.
Forgive that internal being that you know so well.
Forgive the thoughtless mistakes that are part of the whole
Of the internal being.

Laugh within..
Laugh at the serious and vulnerable within you.
Laugh at the pride that keeps you anxious.
Laugh at the fear that holds you back.

Love completely.
Love the internal self.
Love the deep inner being that is you.

Appreciate the creator of you and your life.
Appreciate your body.
Appreciate the created world in which your body lives
In harmony, symbiotically.

Believe.
Send joy to the universe.
Send love to the world.
Believe that the love you send impacts creation
*

WHEN MAEVE WAS 3
SHE ASKED ME
WHO IS GOD?

WELL, I REALLY DIDN'T KNOW.

NOW SHE IS 5.
I HAVE STUDIED, READ
AND THOUGHT.

GOD IS THE MYSTERY THAT
EVERY MAN RECOGNIZES.

GOD IS JUST THAT -
    THE UNKNOWABLE
    UNNAMABLE
      INDESCRIBABLE
MYSTERY

AT THE CENTER OF ALL CREATION
*

On Making Decisions

Make those little decisions!
Be bold!
Have fun!

Decide on the color to polish your nails.
Choose carefully from the dinner menu.
Select your friends with thoughtfulness.
Adjust the pillows.
Rearrange the furniture.

Make those little decisions!
With flair!
With joy and laughter!

For in every day, a person
really cannot make a life affecting decision.

Your health,
your soul's work,
your unexpected troubles
are
at
the
whim
of
another
decision
maker.
*

Tightly Wrapped

Some things are fine wrapped tightly.

A baby in a blanket swaddled
close feels snug, secure.
A present wrapped with care
and the delight of anticipation
for the receiver's surprise,
the giver's delight.
A sandwich made fresh this
morning, tightly packaged
in plastic wrap.

Other things are better loosely held.

Love.
Relationships.
Ideas.
The certainty of our beliefs.
*

A Poem for My Friend in Sorrow

I would cover your shoulders with the cloak
of familiarity.
Keep you warm in the comfort of
my arms.
Bring you soup from the stove of
lost desires and rekindle
the soft glow of serenity.
I would plump your pillows behind your back.
Pillows filled with memories
that support you.
Place your feet on the footstool of love.
Surround you with flowers whose perfume
would give
certainty, security, and calmness.

I cannot take your grief away
but, oh, I am by your side.
*

The Sparrow

In the warm library,
at church,
this morning,
we talked about
Sarah and Hagar,
Abraham and Lot.

Driving,
the back roads home,
I saw,
a hawk,
swoop across.
the road,
in front of my car.

We talked about God,
and how Abraham
could know
it was God speaking.

A tiny sparrow flew before the hawk.
Flew into the vastness of the open space called road,
hoping to reach the protection of the trees,
I guess.

Sarah and Hagar,
mothers of nations,
used,
abused,
a part of nature.

With a spectacular show of wings and feathers,
the hawk grabbed the sparrow in its talons.

I drove on home
down the frosty, cold
road.
*

God's there

God's there,
but where?

Whose hands can God use,
if not mine?

Stories, fellowship,
activities,
God's seen in
every one of these.

But now, retired,
learning on my own,
I find that God is here and now
in every aging bone.

God laughs with me and
and feels my pain,
God sings to me,
and wakes my brain,

God loves with me,
and often may
look askance at things I say.

I find god now inside of me
as God is in each thing I see.
*

Where Are the Prophets?

Who changes our world today?
Who calls out to us to see the big issues?
Issues lurk under petty details
like Aconites peek forth
from a blanket of old snow?
Where are the prophets?

Sexuality catches our attention.
But where are the prophets?
Telling others how to think is our way.
But where are the prophets?
Collecting our goods,
keeping our silence,
hanging on to our treasured way
of looking at issues, we do.

We are forgetting to look for the prophets.
We are forgetting to expect change.
We are forgetting how universal God is.

Like the Aconites,
peeping above the old snow,
so must we peep above our blanket of silliness,
to grow.

Peek up from under the clutter of wetness and mud,
and look for the prophets who will bring us
the ideas we long to reach toward.

Call louder prophets of today.
Listen harder souls to what they say.
*

The Veil in America

When women wear the veil,
covered by the chador,
it may be, as for the Grandmothers,
a contract with God,
a celebration of their
relationship with God.

Or, if the regime in power dictates,
what of the veil?
What does the chador conceal?
Women's wantonness?
Men's desires?
Primitive possession of purity?

Is it power that the symbol of the veil declares?
Women, are you under man's control?

And , in America, do we less than
our Muslim sisters, use our
veils of foundation, rouge,
dye, and powder, gloss and color?

Are our veils, that mark us,
subservient to the
hopes and expectations of our
males?

The difference may seem to be choice,
our freedom to choose versus the regime
dictations,
But, do we dance with the jailer, sisters?
*

The Mark of Cain

In Bible days, tribes had marks,
tattoo's to mark their members.
The "law of blood revenge" was
used.
Your tribal mark protected you.

To be alone in the desert without a
a tribal mark
meant death. The "mark of
Cain" was God's protection.

Today, the baseball caps, the colored
shirt, the hand signs
swiftly given,
mark for the urban child a safety
zone where blood
revenge protects them.

And where is God, both then and now?
How does God's love protect us?
Compassion, relationship,
outward signs,
or can faith alone shield us?
*

Creation Midrash

Genesis 1:26 and 27, Genesis 2:7
*Let us make human kind in our image...
so God created humankind
male and female he created them
...the Lord God formed man from the dust of the ground.*

With reverence,
God
placed the humankind,
male and female as they were created,
back on the breast of their mother
to be nurtured and fed. And their mother,
earth and planet,
nature, calm and stormy,
nurtured her children with abundance.

Lavishly,
the mother, earth,
nourished her children with spring water,
green growing plants,
and animal companions of every kind.

Lovingly,

the mother, planet,
provided weather and protection from the weather,
storms to clear the trees of dead branches,
lightening fires to bring the forest re-birth,
and climates of every variety for her children, humankind.

Loyally,
the mother, nature,
provided for the reproduction of her children,
fostering progeny for all living things,
beginning fresh with each new generation
for continuance of life.

And,
like all mothers,
she provided unselfish love,
constant reassurance,
and forgiveness
accompanied by the teachings of a better way.

Care for the earth;
she who gave you birth
who sustains your life on earth.

With reverence were we laid
upon the earth who paid
with ravaged soil
with craters caused by war
with the ceaseless selfishness of those she bore.

Oh Mother Earth
Oh God in Heaven
Oh people here in life...

Compassion comes with empathy.
Compassion for the earth you see.
Compassion starts within
the hearts of
only you and *only* me.
*

At Crack of Dawn

At crack of dawn,
I took the Buddhist path.
At noon,
I walked with Christ.
By evening Yahweh led
me through the wilderness
with Abraham.
And when the darkness came,
Ishmael held my hand.

Through the night,
I wrestled with angels,
spirits, avatars.

The Divine, the Eternal,
the Mystery of thinking man,
begins the compassion
that starts within each soul,
and has no end.
*

Of Nature

Part Three

Daylight

When the bug lit on my page
he cast a shadow
defined by the bright sunlight.

His shadow clearly showed his stinger.
A stinging bug.
His stinger most clear in shadow as he was
a translucent brown and golden bug,
nondescript against the page,

but the shadow of the tail piece
was a contrast of sharp black
against white.

One marvels at
the sun and light
and how it throws
a shadow bright
into a focus that is
piercingly hard to see in broad daylight.
*

Silence

Some kinds of silence are
so deep that they
allow you to hear everything.

The silence by the side of a lake
unruffled by breezes or men

The silence of the darkness
uncluttered by daily sound

The silence of the moment
after something wrong
was said

Then, tiny noises begin to come
like the wings in flight
of the hummingbird's hum

The knock of woodpecker
on the tree

The altering sound of the
buzzing bee

The splash in the lake that
was a frog on the shore

The beaver's tail against
the water warning evil
from his door.

Some kinds of silence are
so clear that they allow
you to hear, even your deepest fear.
*

A Thought of Conservation

What is the true death?
Is it not extinction?
When all mankind is gone
there will be
No immortality through progeny.

So, truly, does procreation
ward off the worms of death,
the maggots everlasting?

Perhaps, now think,
the true triumph
over death is to
leave the planet earth with
abundance for all living creatures -
men, plants, animals, God.

So, not by progeny alone
are we immortalized,
But through serving
the earthly abundance that
we have been given.

To pass it on, forever.

The Sky Hangs Heavy with Gray

The sky hangs heavy with gray.
The clouds are full.
Expectant.
Waiting above to let
the nourishing moisture
fall to the earth.
Lovingly.

Little flakes of snow
Small, dense,
Begin to descend from the gray clouds.
filling the cracks in the frozen
grass, over the single blades.
Covering the bumpy earth with purity.
Oneness.

The blanket of purity
so deep today, will melt, slowly,
and the face of the earth,
fertile and fecund
will appear again with
the cracks, the valleys,
the blades of grass showing in the lawn.
Individually.
*

The trees that block the view...
Do they enclose me in nature?
Or prevent me from seeing
   the reality of the distance?

*

The Muse

It must be the rain
that brings out the muse
who sings in me today.

The subtle rumbling of
the thunder.
The shifting changes of humidity.
The air that sits heavier
than on a sunny day.

Welcome muse!
Though I be weary, sad, or ill,
I'll welcome you
and do my best your lovely soul to fill.
*

Sons of Thunder- Daughters of the Mist

Like fury came the sound of rain and
with it came the thunder.

Following, the mist arose.
With gentle touch,
it folded
in the noise of force.

Calm is strength beyond the
loud,
when life is lived
without the shroud of death.

How do we resolve the
images given by the cloud
of rain and mist and fog and force?

While humans here on earth we
are wrapped with forces of
all kinds,
striving for the mist,
secure within the thunder.
*

Abraham's Wish

Three silos stood in the field
to the left of the highway.
Together, silver in the
sun.
Three different heights
they were.
Storing three different crops,
perhaps.
Yet each gleaming with sun
reflection
in harmony,
One, with the other,
with the other.
*

Mazatlan

Reuben says you can only
catch Dorado in blue
water.

Green water, beautiful and mystic
undulates close to the shore - foaming,
sparkling, teeming
with small things of the sea.

Blue water, deep and mystic
surges with swells and waves - dark, reflective,
holding the great mysteries of the sea.

Reuben says you can only
catch Dorado in blue water.

Sylvia tells of a shoreline where
you can catch all manner of things -
clues, perhaps,
necessary to unlock the great mysteries of the
blue water sea.
*

The Softness of Spring

Just a little bit of air floats by me.
A soft bit of air.
It gently wafts over my forearms.
It slows my breathing.
It balances on the tops of my bare feet for
just a moment.

The sweetness of the air is in its gentleness.
And also in its fragrance.
Spring, bringing balls of white blossoms on bushes
and puffs of red color on trees.

It makes me lazy.
It reminds me of infants.
It stirs my heart with newness.
It changes the stark outline of winter
Into the softly rolling curves of spring.

This gentle air is open to all.
The circumstances of your being,
and the place you are, matter not
to the gentle touch of spring.
Spring will find you.

The gentlest of days
caresses me,
changing my protective posture, of defense
from cold,
into the open softness and vulnerability to
love
that only spring can offer.
*

Spring Storm

I can hear the storms coming.
The birds call more persistently.
The tops of the trees blow in different directions
at the same time - causing a whooshing noise
that whispers "storm ahead".

I can smell the storm coming.
Faint smell of rain intermittent on the
variable winds.
Heavy smell of blossoms ripe on the trees
between puffs of breeze.

I can see the storm coming.
Change in light.
Gray takes over blazing blue.
Soft, hazy aspirations of shadows and shade.

I can taste the storm, salty
from drops of drying sweat in the air
that rests heavy with heat.

But I cannot touch the storm.
*

In the City

The sun cut across my backyard.
It raced around the corner of
the building next door
Leaving me, once again in,
the dim light.

I tried to find it - hurrying
to my front door.
It winked at me, once, quickly,
as the gray clouds covered
the burst of rays.

To seek the sun requires
planning and attention.
It is not random.

To find the sun,
unexpectedly,
unbidden,
shining through the
tall buildings, landing on
a patch of worn brick,
Ah, to find the sun, unexpectedly,
is a true gift in the city.
*

Choices

A thinning woods
with large patches
of Mayflowers
looking like umbrellas
over a village of teeming life.

While dandelions choose
the sun with bursts
of yellow, calling one.

The daffodils are planted as though
someone placed them there
against the fence,
by the wide front porch.
Their fragrance fills the air.

Which would we choose to be
shade, sun, or tamed?
These, spring's choices, that we see.

*

The Midwest

the trees stand up
on the bare earth
like tufts of hair

grouped together
not too tall
sitting in the midst of
cornfield meadows
of the mid-west

Solid, if not majestic.
Reliable, if not dramatic.
*

Many Layers Showing

Dressed in shades of green,
their sparkling shoulders
dipping with the wind,
offering come hither calls to those of us
enclosed
in our protective walls...
the trees.

Clad in blouses with puffed sleeves,
gauzy blouses blown by breeze,
Covered by a skirt in greys
against the blue background skies
on mostly sunny days...
the clouds.

Surrounded by petticoats in
many layers showing under
skirts of green-blue ocean's waves
of ruffles
move past lands of sandy hues...
the waves.

Each dress of nature lovely.
Each ensemble fit for a queen.
But, my favorite, brilliant favorite,
is the sunset rarely seen in pinks,
golds, purples, fiery reds, pale blues,
the sunset revealing of the splendor,
given to us through earthly clues.

A gown of color that reflects the mystery,
that covers the unknown, a sunset of our own.
*

With Relationships

Part Four

Old Marriages

Old marriages ebb and flow.
That seems to be what they are about.
Old marriages.
They ebb and flow.

A sharp word here, that
slaps like a cold wave
against your ankle
on the warm beach.

Then the sand warms
up your toes again and
on down the level
beach you walk,
for a while..

A rogue wave may have built
over time out on the cold
and lonesome sea.
From the sea, coming
to the shore as a tsunami,
requiring the cleansing
of the aftermath of
storm's rage by careful persistence.

An old marriage knows how
to handle these things.
Recognizing the ebb and flow.
Clashing on the shore
to delve back into the ocean,
to bring the security of warm sand
on the journey forward.

Comfort in strength.
Comfort in longevity.
Challenges met.
And re-met and re-met.
They ebb and flow.
Old marriages.
*

The Two of Us

I lock the doors.
It helps me to unwind.
You unlock the doors.
Locks feel like
ties that bind.

I wash your shirts.
I like the fresh clean smell.
You like the shirts that
hang on chairs, their
wrinkles drape so well.

I set the table with
a small bouquet.
You mound your plate
and go to what ever is on the old TV.

You turn the radio up.
I turn the radio off.

You generously offer me your toothbrush,
for my forgotten one.
I holler, lordy me, you have forgotten that its
me.

For never under any sun
do you and I appear as one,
but each of us, as both we are,
together make one over par.
*

Chalking the Walk

The bums, you know,
would come around.
They had a secret system
of marking sidewalks.
Using charcoal they would put
a certain mark if you
were generous with food.
But a different mark they'd make,
if you were not inclined to share your take.

They would also warn
each other of dogs.

Gramma didn't mind the bums at first,
finding bread or meat leftovers
to share
Eventually, though, she learned of
the chalk marks on the walk
and began her generosity to despair.

Watch out for bums! Hobos from
the train! They'll eat you
out of house and home and
send back friends again.
*

A Bit of Space

There should remain, between the generations,
Mother and daughter,
A bit of space.

Some thoughts do not need to be shared to keep an
honest relationship.

Some relationships can be honest only if some
Thoughts are not shared.

There is a realm of polite, gracious silence
where mothers and daughters can walk together.
Maybe it is pretend.
Maybe it is the only reality on earth
that sustains and nourishes a lifelong
relationship.

Between the generations, mother and daughter,
There is an understanding that is deeper
than the neon lights of absolute truth and
sharing.

A bit of space between the generations may be the
rich earth that fertilizes
the germinating seeds of completeness, one
with the other.

Mother, a source and beginning.
Daughter, a continuing hope.

The Grandmothers Thread

I am here because
of the grandmothers
thread.

I am learning to weave
the thread into generations
that follow:
daughters,
grandchildren,
daughters-in-law,
nieces,
friends,
and share and learn from the generations that
are: sisters,
mothers,

grandmothers,
cousins,

sisters-in-law,

friends.

I am only learning
to weave the thread,
I learn some new cross weave
or design every day.

Every day, every day I must
find a way to share
the intricacies of being
a woman.

Sending the grandmothers
thread, out to others,
with love, with comfort,
with strength,
with care,
Uniting women everywhere.

Catching the grandmothers thread
tossed to me
with gratitude unbounded
as I live my life so free.
*

Grief…….

Immense grief leaks out
a little bit at a time.

It drips from your eyes
as you put the tea water on.

It prickles your sinuses
when the sun hits the
porch in the late afternoon..

It wells in your heart,
gathers in your eyes,
And drips down your cheeks,
unbidden

On its own schedule.
In its own time.
Bit by bit.
Never gone.

Can it be a comfort to know
that you are capable
of love so strong that
Love's inevitable partner,
Grief,
makes you vulnerable
to unexpected weeping at the loss?
*

Do Not Be Afraid To Love

Do not be afraid to love,
my child.

Love is hard.
It leaves you vulnerable
to hurt.
It makes you weep.
It tests your patience.
It draws from you depths
of maturity you
did not know you had,
nor do you really want.

Do not be afraid to love,
my child.

There is no other way to reach
the supreme heights,
the extreme depths,
of the true life
that is available to us.

Available to us,
only by loving.

Do not be afraid to love,
My child.
*

Maeve's Magic Wand

The first time I saw you
use a magic wand
we were in China - at a temple.

You and I left the tour and found
a bench with shade for me,
and soft dirt for you.

You found a stick
and you began to play.
You made your stick into wand.
a magic wand.
The magic wand drew a little city
there in the dirt.

You drew small children going to school.
You made a place for a house
where the mother was waiting.
There were dragons.
You changed them to kittens
with your magic wand.

Then, this year, at Easter
you got another magic wand.
You waved it in the air.
You made magic everywhere.

But on a cool spring day,
In the midst of your play,
the wand broke.
The sparkles left.
You were so sad.
You were bereft.

While nothing will replace
that magic wand.
Just like the stick from China
is now gone,
always, Maeve, for you,
there will be magic
hiding
in everything you do.
*

Sustaining

My mother had a stroke.
She cannot eat.
Her nutrition is delivered by
an intravenous drip.

Food is the center of a ritual of love.
We feed each other to mourn.
We feed each other to comfort.

My mother and I have lost our ritual.
I feel without a means to mourn.
I do not know how to comfort her.

Most days are marked by meal times.
We separate the day by segments,
breakfast, lunch and dinner.

I do not know how to help her pass the days.
Time runs together without the ritual.
There is no break for tea.
There is no chance to share
a cookie with our coffee.

Nothing signals morning.
Nothing signals night,
no snack at bedtime to recount the day.

My mother had a stroke.
She cannot eat,
but, I, using all my strength,
I will feed her with my love
*

A Mother's Job
Ironing Out the Wrinkles of Responsibility

She checked the cloth for dampness,
and the iron for heat.
Then, she began to smooth from the wrinkled linen
a small spot of steamy flatness.
Flatness, like
on a quiet lake
on a foggy morning
when the sun rises, a
and a surface patch of flat calmness
appears.

A little dampness, not too wet,
a little heat, not to scorch,
a little steam from the heat and the
dampness,
a little pressure from the iron
as it unites the elements, and wrinkles
begin to meld
into the finished beauty they were
meant to be.

So it is with our children
as they grow.
They need a little dampness,
a little heat,
a few wrinkles
that require the careful touch of intervention
to assist in
smoothing their way.
*

Boys and Girls

The month of May carries a name
that belongs to girls.
May.

Merry month.
Fertile month.
New births.

An open month is May.
Open your hearts.
Open your windows.
Open your arms.

The month of August carries a boy's name.

Transition month.
Dying month.
Leave takings.

A closed month is August.
Close the summer silliness.
Close your windows.
Close your stores for winter.

How sweet can spring be without the cold contrast
of the ice and the battle fought so bravely to survive?

The girls may lead the merry chase,
But boys must eagerly pursue,
To bring to life the future race,
And present to spring its due.
*

Centered

I have a friend whose
life is like a landscape.
Trees, flowers, shrubs,
green growing things
for beauty,
green growing things
for nourishment -
All growing things honored and
loved and cherished.

Now, at a certain age, my friend
is clearing the
landscape of her life -
a bit.
Taking out one or two things,
reorganizing a center clearing
leaving a patch to lie fallow
in the sunshine, the rain,
the frost, the snow,
the cool rays of moonlight.

And watching, waiting expectantly -
What will grow next?
What will grow next?